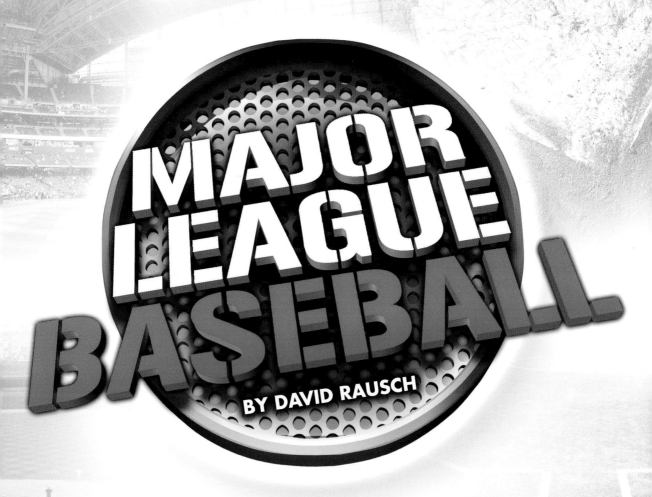

MAJOR LEAGUE BASEBALL

BY DAVID RAUSCH

BELLWETHER MEDIA • MINNEAPOLIS, MN

EPIC BOOKS are no ordinary books. They burst with intense action, high-speed heroics, and shadows of the unknown. Are you ready for an Epic adventure?

This edition first published in 2015 by Bellwether Media, Inc.

No part of this publication may be reproduced in whole or in part without written permission of the publisher. For information regarding permission, write to Bellwether Media, Inc., Attention: Permissions Department, 5357 Penn Avenue South, Minneapolis, MN 55419.

Library of Congress Cataloging-in-Publication Data

Rausch, David.
  Major League Baseball / by David Rausch.
    pages cm. – (Epic: Major League Sports)
  Includes bibliographical references and index.
  Summary: "Engaging images accompany information about Major League Baseball. The combination of high-interest subject matter and light text is intended for students in grades 2 through 7"– Provided by publisher.
  ISBN 978-1-62617-133-6 (hardcover : alk. paper)
  1. Major League Baseball (Organization)–Juvenile literature. 2. Baseball–United States–Juvenile literature. 3. Major League Baseball–Juvenile literature. 4. Major League Baseball–History–Juvenile literature. I. Title.
  GV875.A1R38 2014
  796.357'64–dc23
                        2014009653

Printed in the United States of America, North Mankato, MN.

TABLE OF CONTENTS

WHAT IS MLB?

Major **League** Baseball (MLB) brings together **professional** baseball teams in North America. Ball players from all over the world play in MLB.

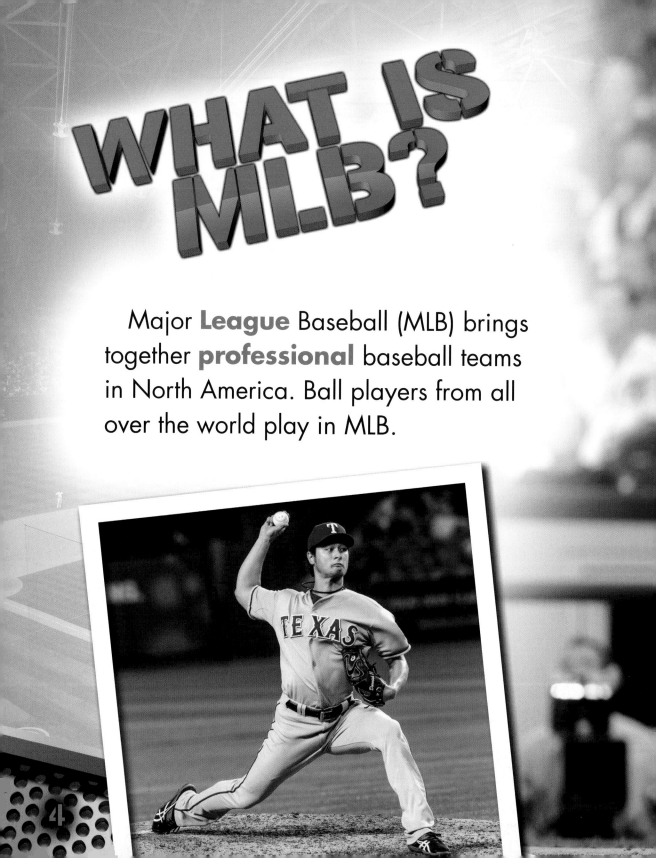

HISTORY OF MLB

The Cincinnati Red Stockings became the first professional baseball team in 1869. Eventually the team moved from Ohio to Boston. They formed the National Association (NA) with eight other teams.

FIRST NINE OF THE
CINCINNATI
(RED STOCKINGS) BASE BALL CLUB.

FIRST WORLD SERIES

In 1903, the best NL and AL teams played each other. The Boston Pilgrims won five games to beat the Pittsburgh Pirates.

The National League (NL) took shape in 1876. It replaced the NA. The NL had control of the baseball scene until the American League (AL) formed in 1901. Two years later, the NL and AL became MLB.

A LOOK BACK

1869: The Cincinnati Red Stockings become the first professional baseball team.

March 17, 1871: The first league forms. It is called the National Association.

February 2, 1876: The National League forms.

January 28, 1901: The American League forms.

August 3, 1903: The NL and AL join to form Major League Baseball.

October 10, 1903: The Boston Pilgrims beat the Pittsburgh Pirates in the first World Series.

July 6, 1933: The best NL and AL players compete in the first All-Star Game.

June 12, 1939: The Baseball Hall of Fame opens in Cooperstown, New York.

August 26, 1939: An MLB game is on television for the first time.

April 15, 1947: Jackie Robinson becomes the first African-American to play in an MLB game.

June 8, 1965: The first MLB draft takes place. Rick Monday is picked first.

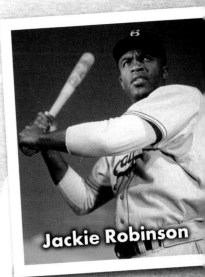

Jackie Robinson

THE TEAMS

MLB has 30 teams. They belong to either the NL or AL. Each league has three **divisions** of 5 teams.

AL. NL.

American League Central

- **Chicago White Sox**
- **Cleveland Indians**
- **Detroit Tigers**
- **Kansas City Royals**
- **Minnesota Twins**

National League Central

- **Chicago Cubs**
- **Cincinnati Reds**
- **Milwaukee Brewers**
- **Pittsburgh Pirates**
- **St. Louis Cardinals**

American League East

- **Baltimore Orioles**
- **Boston Red Sox**
- **New York Yankees**
- **Tampa Bay Rays**
- **Toronto Blue Jays**

National League East

- **Atlanta Braves**
- **Miami Marlins**
- **New York Mets**
- **Philadelphia Phillies**
- **Washington Nationals**

American League West

- **Houston Astros**
- **Los Angeles Angels of Anaheim**
- **Oakland Athletics**
- **Seattle Mariners**
- **Texas Rangers**

National League West

- **Arizona Diamondbacks**
- **Colorado Rockies**
- **Los Angeles Dodgers**
- **San Diego Padres**
- **San Francisco Giants**

BATTER UP!

Only the AL uses a Designated Hitter (DH). The DH bats for the pitcher.

Each team has an **active roster** of 25 men. Teams pick up **free agents**, **draft** new players, and trade players. They also call players up from the **minor leagues**.

MLB draft

PLAYING THE GAME

Each **inning**, both teams bat and play defense. They switch places after three outs. **Umpires** decide who is out. After nine innings, the team with the most runs wins!

umpire ——

EXTRA INNINGS

A tie game goes into extra innings. Play continues until one team wins. The longest MLB game lasted 26 innings.

BASEBALL TALK

ball—when a pitch misses the strike zone and the batter does not swing at the ball

base hit—when the batter hits the ball and reaches first base safely

foul ball—when a ball is hit into foul territory; foul territory is the part of the field outside the first and third base foul lines.

out—when the batter or runner must return to the bench without scoring

run—when the batter reaches all four bases and scores

strike—when a pitch enters the strike zone or the batter swings and misses the ball; the strike zone is an area above home plate.

strikeout—when a pitcher throws three strikes; 1 out

walk—when a pitcher throws four balls and sends the batter to first base

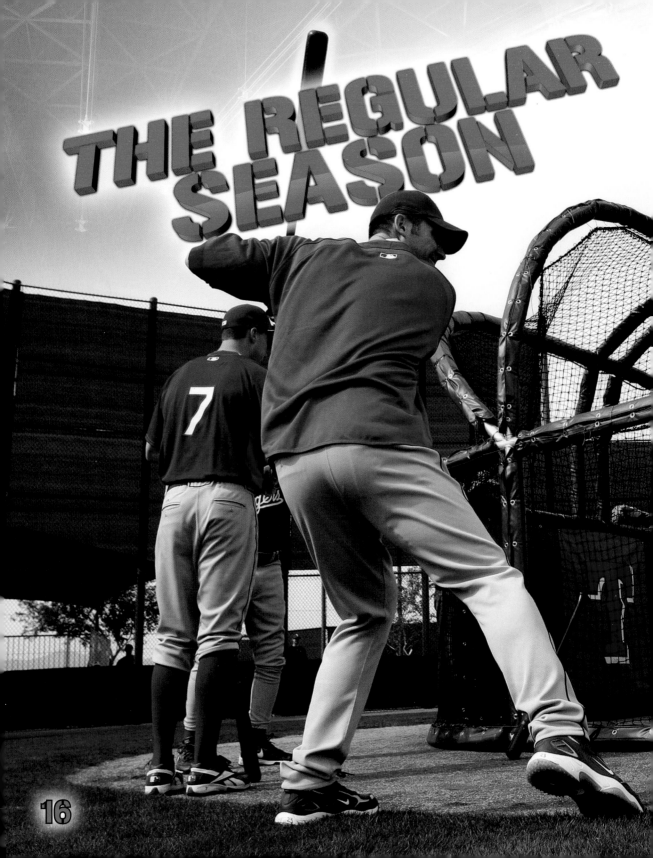

THE REGULAR SEASON

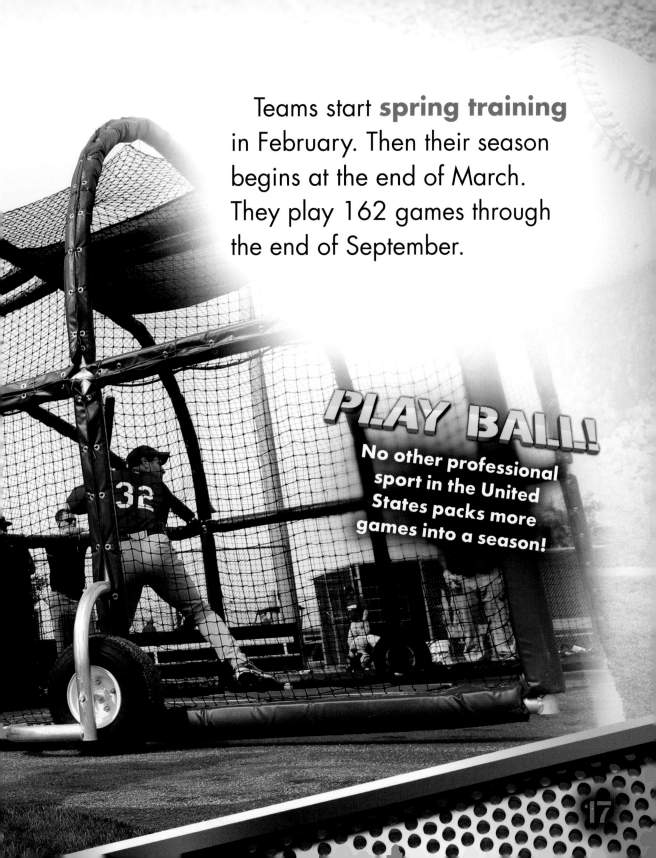

Teams start **spring training** in February. Then their season begins at the end of March. They play 162 games through the end of September.

PLAY BALL!

No other professional sport in the United States packs more games into a season!

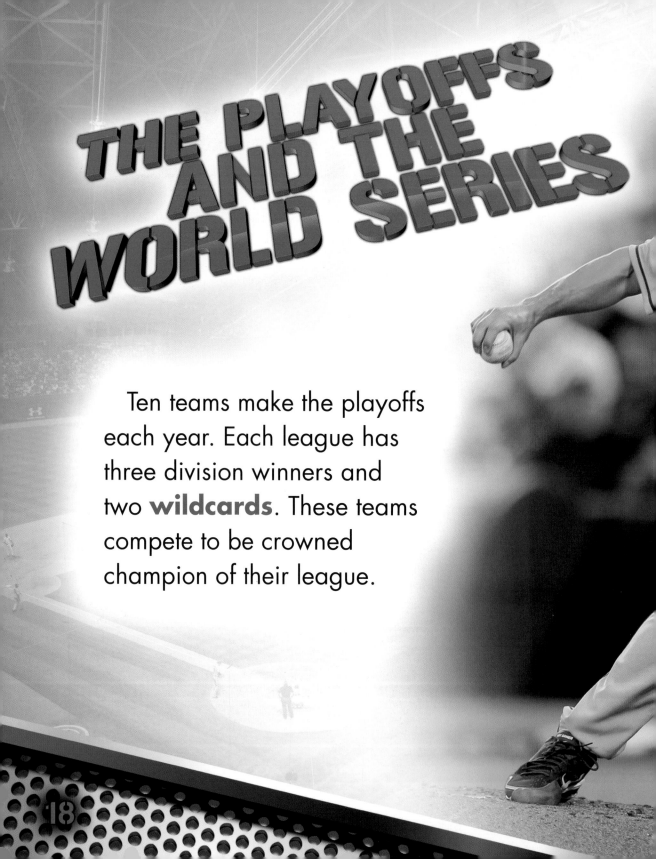

THE PLAYOFFS AND THE WORLD SERIES

Ten teams make the playoffs each year. Each league has three division winners and two **wildcards**. These teams compete to be crowned champion of their league.

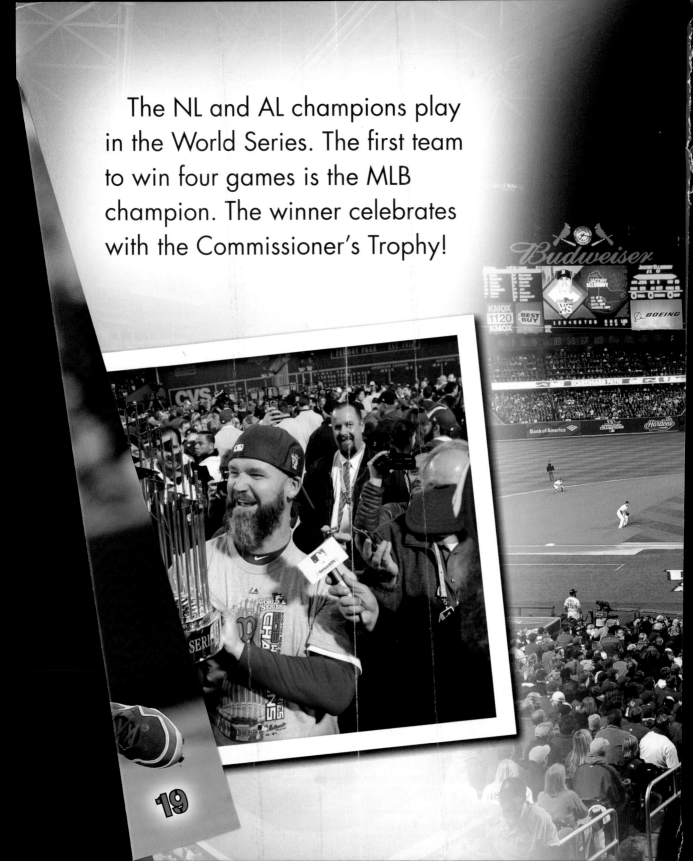

The NL and AL champions play in the World Series. The first team to win four games is the MLB champion. The winner celebrates with the Commissioner's Trophy!

19

THE FALL CLASSIC

The World Series is also called the Fall Classic. This is because it takes place in October.

GLOSSARY

active roster—a list of players on a team who can play in an MLB game

divisions—groups of sports teams within a league; teams in a division often play one another.

draft—to choose players from college teams and the minor leagues to join MLB

free agents—professional athletes who are free to play for any team; free agents do not have contracts.

inning—one of nine periods of time in a baseball game

league—a group of people or teams united by a common interest or activity

minor leagues—lower-level teams that have contracts with major league teams; players can move from the minor leagues to the major leagues.

professional—at a level where athletes get paid to play a sport

spring training—a period of time when teams train for the regular season

umpires—people who enforce the rules during baseball games

wildcards—teams that make the playoffs without winning their division

TO LEARN MORE

At the Library

Borden, Louise. *Baseball Is...* New York, N.Y.: Margaret K. McElderry Books/Simon and Schuster Children's Pub. Division, 2014.

Hetrick, Hans. *Play Baseball Like a Pro: Key Skills and Tips.* Mankato, Minn.: Capstone Press, 2011.

Latimer, Clay. *VIP Pass to a Pro Baseball Game Day: From the Locker Room to the Press Box (and Everything in Between).* Mankato, Minn.: Capstone Press, 2011.

On the Web

Learning more about Major League Baseball is as easy as 1, 2, 3.

1. Go to www.factsurfer.com.

2. Enter "Major League Baseball" into the search box.

3. Click the "Surf" button and you will see a list of related web sites.

With factsurfer.com, finding more information is just a click away.

INDEX